Excellence
PRANAY

BUDDHA
WISDOM LIBRARY

T0349328

Published by

FiNGERPRINT!
Prakash Books

 Fingerprint Publishing
 @FingerprintP
 @fingerprintpublishingbooks
www.fingerprintpublishing.com

Copyright © 2024 Prakash Books
Copyright Text © Pranay Gupta

All rights reserved. No part of this publication may be reproduced, stored in a retrieval system or transmitted in any form or by any means, electronic, mechanical, photocopying, recording or otherwise (except for mentions in reviews or edited excerpts in the media) without the written permission of the publisher.

The views and opinions expressed in this book are solely those of the author. The facts presented were reported as true by the author at the time of publication. The publisher assumes no responsibility for their accuracy or veracity and is not liable for any errors, omissions, or consequences arising from the use of the information. References to third-party products, services, or websites are for informational purposes only and do not constitute endorsements.

ISBN: 978 93 6214 575 8

Remembering our Buddha-nature
takes us toward excellence.

OM MANI PADME HUM

*Remain where you are and apply yourself
diligently to your tasks.*
—Gautam Buddha

*Have a mind that is open to everything,
and attached to nothing.*
—Tilopa's MahamudraTeachings

*Deep within the cave of your heart,
is where all Buddhas unite!*
—Milarepa of Tibet

Contents

1. Zen Attitudes for Excellence   9

2. The Pursuit of Excellence in Buddhism   15

3. 24 Buddhist Secrets for Excellent and Purposeful Living   19

4. Unleashing Excellence: The Buddhist Principle of Detachment   25

5. Pathways to Excellence: Key Principles from Buddhist Scriptures   27

6. Discovering the Inner Gold: The Essence of Buddhism   31

7. 24 Mystical Realizations and Practices for Excellence   33

8. Buddhist Concepts for Excellence   41

9. Principles for Excellence: A Path to Personal and Spiritual Growth   47

10. The Path to Excellence: Insights from the
    Buddha   53

11. Appamāda: Diligence or Zeal in Buddhism   57

12. The Path of Dharma: Cultivating
    Excellence in Life   59

13. Buddhist Keys for Mystic and Material
    Excellence   63

14. Taoism and Buddhism   69

15. The Inner Conquest: Unlocking
    Fulfillment and True Leadership on
    the Path of Gautam Buddha   73

16. Pathways to Enlightenment   79

17. Emulating the Bodhisattvas for Excellence   83

18. The Ultimate Mystic Principles
    for Excellence   93

19. Being Full-hearted: Pour Your Heart!   101

20. Three Teachings for Excellence   111

21. Buddhism's Essence: A Path to Excellence   115

Acknowledgments   129

CHAPTER 1

Zen Attitudes for Excellence

In Japan's Zen Buddhism, it is said that our true nature is like the sky: vast and pristine. Yet, just as clouds can obscure the sky's blueness and vastness, so too can our true nature—our Buddha nature—be clouded by wrong concepts and attitudes. Zen teaches us ways to identify with our inherently excellent, luminous, brilliant

Buddha nature. By recognizing and embracing the natural and true state of the mind, we can attain excellence spontaneously!

Zen Buddhism has inspired several teachings that guide us toward this path of excellence:

A. WABI SABI

The attitude or worldview of Wabi Sabi encourages us to ground ourselves in the natural simplicity of our being. As the Buddha taught, this Zen principle advises us not to be carried away by an obsession with material things but to understand that imperfection and impermanence are inherent in all things. By embracing this concept, our mindset becomes natural and holistic, helping us manage life's challenges and achieve excellence in all areas of our lives (spiritual, material, emotional, relational, etc.).

The key problem is that our minds get clouded by wrong concepts. Life and existence are inherently imperfect, but there is perfection within that imperfection. This understanding aligns us with our Buddha nature and the cosmic mystic law. An excellent example of Wabi Sabi is the practice of Kintsugi, where broken ceramics are repaired and transformed into beautiful pieces. Normally, we might discard broken ceramics, but Kintsugi regards the damage and cracks as beautiful. Understanding this beauty of imperfection helps us establish ourselves in the present moment, embracing our Buddha nature's natural and simple brilliance. This mindset leads us gradually toward excellence.

B. KAIZEN

The second concept, Kaizen, is derived from *Zen* and means continuous improvement. It encourages us to focus on making small, incremental improvements every day. Instead of striving for significant changes simultaneously, we are advised to pursue marginal improvements. This approach allows us to move toward excellence spontaneously, happily, and calmly. Through consistent, small steps, we can achieve excellence naturally and effortlessly.

In other words, we must take small steps, and we will find that we can reach our destination and achieve an excellent way of living life in all dimensions very rapidly! Haste only makes waste. Zen tells us that we need to slow down and become established in the present moment. By doing so, we become better and better every day.

C. SHOSHIN

The third concept in Zen that leads us toward excellence is *Shoshin* or the *beginner's mind*. In Zen, it is said that an empty mind opens up to everything. Zen emphasizes the beginner's mind, meaning we should discard our conditioned notions and remain open. This openness can lead to significant leaps in our perception of things. Once established in the right perception, our consciousness operates at its best, allowing us to think and act more effectively and excellently.

How our consciousness works is the basis of excellence, and this is a primary concern of Zen.

D. IKIGAI

Another crucial concept for excellence is Ikigai, a term that has gained popularity in modern times. Ikigai means living purposefully. It implies doing what we love, what we are good at, what the world needs, and what can provide material, aesthetic, and spiritual value.

Living a purpose-driven life enables us to achieve excellence in all spheres.

Overall, Zen encourages us to adopt certain attitudes and develop a knack for them, making them habits in our lives. By doing so, we spontaneously move toward the all-round excellence the Buddhas have spoken about.

E. HARA HACHI BU

The fifth concept, Hara Hachi Bu, means stopping eating when 80% full. Overeating makes us tired, creates brain fog, and makes us indecisive. While this principle applies to food, it also applies more broadly to everything. We should not constantly hanker after more but live lives of contentment without overstuffing ourselves.

In today's world, it is easy to overindulge, but we need space for our consciousness to operate at its best. This principle helps us live lives of spontaneous excellence, aligning with the very basis of Gautam Buddha's teachings.

CHAPTER 2

The Pursuit of Excellence in Buddhism

From the Buddha's perspective, the dynamic pursuit of excellence is a crucial part of our universal journey. It involves nurturing virtuous qualities and striving to do good deeds in our thoughts, words, and actions.

Excellence in Buddhism is not about perfectionism or achieving superiority over others but rather about striving to develop one's innate potential for goodness and wisdom. It involves cultivating qualities such as compassion, loving kindness, generosity, patience, and wisdom.

The Buddha emphasized the importance of the right effort, one of the factors of the Noble Eightfold Path, in the pursuit of excellence. Right effort involves the diligent cultivation of wholesome qualities and the abandonment of unwholesome tendencies. It entails the effort to prevent the emergence of unwholesome states, to overcome unwholesome states that have already arisen, to cultivate wholesome states, and to maintain and deepen wholesome states that have already been cultivated.

Excellence also involves the practice of mindfulness, another factor of the Noble Eightfold Path, which entails being present and aware in each moment, observing the mind and its contents without judgment or attachment. Through mindfulness, individuals can develop clarity of mind and insight into the true nature of reality, leading to greater wisdom and understanding.

Furthermore, excellence in Buddhism includes living by ethical principles, such as the Five

Precepts, which are guidelines for moral conduct aimed at minimizing harm to oneself and others. By living a virtuous and ethical life, individuals create the conditions for inner peace, harmony, and spiritual growth.

In summary, excellence from the Buddha's perspective involves cultivating wholesome qualities, diligently overcoming unwholesome tendencies, practicing mindfulness and wisdom, and adhering to ethical principles. Through the pursuit of excellence, individuals can progress toward liberation and ultimately achieve lasting happiness and freedom from suffering.

CHAPTER 3

24 Buddhist Secrets for Excellent and Purposeful Living

1. **Quieting the Mind:** Quieting the mind allows the inner Buddha to surface, leading to a fulfilled life.

2. **Path of Love:** Making love the center of one's being brings inner strength, meditativeness, focus, and enlightenment.

3. **Beyond Doubt:** Going beyond doubt and cultivating trust and faith make everything possible in life.

4. **Surrender:** Surrendering to cosmic energy leads to meditation, inner joy, and the discovery of the Buddha within.

5. **Authenticity:** Being oneself, free from masks, brings spontaneous joy, akin to a child's playfulness.

6. **Inner Potential:** Recognizing the mystical power within leads to a transformed perspective on life's value.

7. **River of Desire:** Crossing the river of material desires leads to true happiness and delight.

8. **Pure Witness:** Becoming a pure witness fosters non-attachment and gives rise to virtues like compassion and empathy.

9. **Present-Moment Awareness:** Establishing oneself in the present moment creates crystal-clear lucidity, joy, and true happiness.

10. **Vast Existence:** Developing a vaster vision provides strength, liberating individuals from boundaries and limitations.

11. **Spiritual Rebirth:** Giving up the known and being reborn spiritually leads to courage, happiness, and bliss.

12. **Renouncing the Past:** The true Buddhist spirit is defined as moving forward without carrying the burden of the past.

13. **Moving Beyond Comfort Zones:** Going beyond comfort zones and looking at the higher transforms individuals into mature beings.

14. **Sorrows and Spiritual Growth:** Unhappiness can lead to spiritual growth and a thirst for freedom.

15. **Freedom from Belief Systems:** Freedom from belief systems and ideologies paves the way for deeper meditation and purposeful living.

16. **Knowing Yourself:** Buddhism is about self-understanding, leading to bliss and a sense of purpose.

17. **Brotherhood of Humanity:** Beyond divisions, Buddhism emphasizes the brotherhood of humanity, promoting a better world.

18. **Totality of Intelligence:** True brilliance involves a totality of intelligence, including empathy and the mystical search.

19. **Attaining Wisdom:** Buddhism values attaining wisdom through inner quietness and meditation rather than mere saintliness.

20. **Letting Go of Conditioning:** Letting go of conditioning and being original allows individuals to evolve and grow.

21. **Maturity:** Buddhism encourages spiritual, emotional, and intellectual maturity, moving beyond possessiveness and aggressiveness.

22. **Self-Realization:** The ultimate ambition in Buddhism is self-realization, surpassing all other ambitions.

23. **Questioning Yourself:** The search for answers should come from within through self-questioning and introspection.

24. **Sensitivity and Strength:** Sensitivity to nature and the ability to appreciate beauty make individuals stronger, following the path of the Buddhas.

These teachings offer valuable insights, emphasizing self-awareness, love, compassion, and the pursuit of wisdom for a truly excellent, fulfilling, and purposeful life.

CHAPTER 4

Unleashing Excellence: The Buddhist Principle of Detachment

The Buddhist perspective illuminates a profound truth in pursuing excellence: *true excellence arises from complete non-attachment and non-clinging to results and to things (anupādāna).*

Clinging to (or fixating on) the outcomes of our endeavors shackle us, ensnaring our minds in worries and attachments. We over-worry about potential results, success, and failure, limiting our ability to perform at our best. Trapped in this cycle, we fail to unleash our inherent brilliance.

By embracing detachment from outcomes, we can transcend these constraints and tap into our fullest potential. In Buddhism, when we release our grip on expectations and desires, we liberate ourselves to act with unparalleled freedom and creativity. Detachment empowers us to approach every task with abandon, unencumbered by imagined concerns about outcomes.

Hence, the first secret to achieving excellence lies in cultivating detachment and non-clinging in every aspect of our lives. Doing so unlocks a profound sense of peace amidst even the most demanding endeavors. In embracing detachment, we effortlessly attain excellence and fulfill our inherent potential.

CHAPTER 5

Pathways to Excellence: Key Principles from Buddhist Scriptures

Within the vast teachings of Buddhism lie profound insights guiding the journey toward excellence and enlightenment. Drawing from the scriptures, several essential factors emerge as guiding principles for seekers:

1. **Buddha *Anusatti* (Reflection on Buddha's Qualities):** Mindfully contemplating the virtues of the Buddha awakens similar qualities within us, paving the path toward excellence and enlightenment.

2. **Seven Treasures (*Dhana*):** Embracing these seven qualities accelerates our progress toward excellence in both spiritual and material realms:
   - **Faith:** Trusting in oneself, the Buddha, the *Dhamma*, and the *Sangha* lays the foundation for all subsequent growth.
   - **Good Moral Attitude:** Cultivating virtuous conduct fortifies our inner strength in thoughts, speech, and actions.
   - **Moral Integrity:** Upholding ethics and integrity foster a well-rounded existence.
   - **Avoidance of Harmful Behavior:** Conscious efforts to refrain from causing harm to others reflect our commitment to compassionate living.
   - **Cultivating Wisdom:** Deepening our understanding of the Buddha's teachings enables clarity and insight in navigating life.

- **Generosity:** Embracing selflessness and contributing to others' well-being enriches both our internal being and material potential.
- **Insight:** Prioritizing personal insight gained through meditation empowers us to excel spiritually and in worldly pursuits, moving beyond mere knowledge accumulation.

By integrating these teachings into our lives, we embark on a transformative journey toward holistic excellence, embodying strength, courage, wisdom, and compassion. This multifaceted approach allows us to navigate life's complexities with grace and purpose, leading to profound fulfillment and enlightenment.

CHAPTER 6

Discovering the Inner Gold: The Essence of Buddhism

In Buddhism, the profound wisdom lies in recognizing that the true gold resides within us. Despite our constant external quest, we overlook the 24-karat gold within. We keep striving to *become* something when we are already that something!

This metaphor encapsulates the essence of Buddhism—everything we seek is inherently present within, holding boundless potential for bliss, self-realization, and understanding our own strengths and capabilities. The first step to excellence is realizing your uniqueness. This makes you utterly relaxed within yourself and dynamizes your energy.

Buddhism, at its core, unveils our highest capabilities. This makes it a profoundly practical path to unlocking our inherent potential.

Despite our education and qualifications, we can sometimes fall short of self-actualizing our inherent capabilities. Buddha's philosophy emphasizes unlocking one's potential and transcending limitations. It's about realizing and manifesting your aspirations in life, or your chosen line, like art, business, technology, or any field. The deep introspection and thirst for uncovering your highest capabilities, inherent in Buddhism, yield positive external outcomes. Notably, figures like Steve Jobs found inspiration in Zen Buddhism, highlighting its practical value beyond a mere religious framework.

Buddhism, therefore, offers a profound path to personal and practical fulfillment, as well as deep inner peace and serenity.

24 Mystical Realizations and Practices for Excellence

Continuing the exploration of Buddhist mystic concepts, let us delve into more realizations and practices to manifest excellence in life:

1. **Joy through Meditation:** Buddhism encourages going beyond conditioned

fears and anxieties through pure meditation. Pure joy arises from unfiltered, present-moment experiences, leading to higher happiness.

2. **True Knowing:** True knowing dawns when personal prejudices do not distort reality. The analogy of a sculptor chipping away unnecessary elements from a rock symbolizes the pursuit of pure beauty, strength, calmness, and serenity.

3. **Vast Emptiness:** Buddhism views reality as a vast emptiness (*Shunyata*). Despite existence's transient nature, ineffable beauty can be found even in fleeting moments, akin to appreciating cherry blossoms in Japanese culture.

4. **Order and Balance:** Two crucial elements on the Buddhist path are bringing feelings and thoughts into order and experiencing balance. These aspects complement each other, leading to a perception of reality and attaining great happiness.

5. **Confronting Anxieties:** Buddhism emphasizes confronting anxieties and fears rather than

escaping them. Confrontation dissolves apprehensions, prevents the formation of complexes, and contributes to inner peace.

6. **Walking Lightly:** Buddhism advises looking at and dropping the burdens we carry, walking lightly onward in dynamism. This movement toward inner freedom activates boundless energy, allowing for stillness and dynamism.

7. **Stillness and Dynamism:** The balance of stillness and dynamism allows individuals to go beyond thoughts, images, and ideas, facing reality passionately and unattached. True passion, in the Buddhist view, arises when one is unattached.

8. **Non-Doing:** Buddhism suggests that even in action, there is a non-doer, the essential Buddha nature. Touching this non-doing aspect through silence and contemplation is true meditativeness in all activities, embodying the principles of Karma Yoga.

9. **Graceful Relating:** In Buddhism, the measure of spiritual evolution is how individuals relate

to others and the environment. Graceful and sublime relations indicate a correct consciousness.

10. **Movement of Consciousness:** Buddhism views consciousness as a constantly moving river. Understanding this movement eliminates egoism and identification with the "I," allowing for a renewed relationship with the universe and fearlessness in facing life.

11. **Importance of a Fresh Mind:** Buddhism considers the mind's freshness vital. Clearing the mind of conditioning and adopting a fresh, patternless outlook, as seen in Zen, leads to a psychologically exact and spiritually awakened state.

12. **Pure Perception:** Buddhism asserts that everything in nature rejoices, and pure perception is the essence of Buddhism. Clarity of perception leads to happiness, bliss, delight, joy, love, strength, and inner power.

13. **The Inner Teacher:** While Buddha is the ultimate teacher, Buddhism emphasizes that the ultimate teacher is within oneself. Dependency on external factors limits enlightenment, and realizing the inner Buddha leads to true awakening.

14. **Deep Social and Moral Teaching:** Buddhism's deeply social and moral teachings emphasize helping each other and uniting humanity, making its message relevant in a globalized world.

15. **Be Yourself:** Buddhism highlights the importance of being oneself, aligning with the concept in Hinduism. Being in a state of self-realization allows for the right actions and further progress on the path.

16. **De-Hypnotizing Oneself:** Buddhism calls for de-hypnotizing oneself from past conditioning imposed by religion, society, and culture. Freedom from acquired knowledge is the beginning of the journey toward enlightenment.

17. **Breaking Patterns:** Buddhism advises breaking free from conditioned patterns, as consciousness needs to be free and expansive. A patternless, free mind is essential for attaining Nirvana or complete freedom.

18. **Empathy as a Guide:** The Buddha emphasizes the importance of empathy in guiding others. Empathy fosters the energetic imparting of lessons and arises from real power and heart-to-heart teaching.

19. **Fresh Outlook in Crisis:** Buddhism's relevance in times of crisis lies in adopting a Zen 'beginner's mind.' Discarding previous notions and maintaining a fresh outlook is crucial in addressing disruptions and making the right decisions.

20. **Silence and Power:** Pure silence is considered the essence of Buddhism. Returning to inner silence, beyond the constant noise of the mind, brings power within and enhances the effectiveness of actions.

21. **Rediscovering Innate Powers:** Buddhism asserts that each being already has the capacity for ultimate truth, consciousness, and beauty. The process of Buddhism is a rediscovery of these innate powers.

22. **Non-Dependency:** True Buddhists accept no external authority except the Buddhas and themselves. Equanimity in relating to all beings, regardless of perceived power dynamics, is a sign of true grace.

23. **Non-Clinging:** Buddhism teaches that to be fully alive to consciousness, one must not cling to the things of the world. Going beyond *grasping* material things brings natural bliss and security.

24. **Inner Buddha as Primary Goal:** Regardless of external accomplishments, life is meaningless without finding the inner Buddha within. Living from the inside out, making the inner treasure the primary goal, gives purpose to all accomplishments.

These Buddhist insights provide a comprehensive guide to living a mindful, balanced, and purposefully excellent life.

CHAPTER 8

Buddhist Concepts for Excellence

POWERS

Buddhist tradition and terminology are rich with descriptions of our inherent abilities, often called magical powers or *iddhi*. *Iddhi* symbolizes the mystical potential within us, known as *abhiññā*, highlighting each being's capacity for infinite mystical prowess. However, these abilities primarily focus on inner transformation and progress toward Buddhahood.

Mythologically, Buddhists speak of *atthita-iddhi*, the power to expand and manifest at will; *vikubbana-iddhi*, the power of transformation; *manomaya-iddhi*, the ability to master the mind and have super-conscious abilities to create forms; and *jnana vipariddhi*, the power of penetrating knowledge. Yet, these powers emanate from a concentrated, focused mind that generates positive outcomes for oneself and others. The greatest magical ability lies in transcending life's challenges through Buddhist wisdom, achieving clarity, happiness, and excellence.

Cultivating a mind free from attachments, delusions, and hatred fosters favorable external circumstances and material success. Internally, balance, calmness, spiritual practice, ethical conduct, and compassion toward others are essential. Cultivating a state of nobility or *ariyiddhi* grants inner peace and excellence as value creators worldwide.

THE MORAL COMPASS OF BUDDHISM: CULTIVATING *HIRI OTAPPA* FOR WHOLESOME LIVING

While Buddhism eschews dogmatic morality, it emphasizes the significance of moral conduct in shaping a fulfilling life. Central to this ethos are the twin concepts of *hiri and otappa*, which encompass moral shame and fear of consequences. Moral shame (*hiri*) compels us to refrain from unethical actions, promoting self-restraint and introspection before engaging in any deed. Similarly, the fear of karmic consequences (*otappa*) encourages mindfulness and consideration of how our actions impact others. These principles foster inner harmony and strengthen our moral foundation, cultivating mutual respect, integrity, and responsibility within society.

Upholding moral principles is the bedrock for excellence, promoting a culture of honor and ethical conduct. Embracing *hiri and otappa* guides individuals toward wholesome action and nurtures a culture of moral excellence.

CONSCIOUSNESS AND CHARACTER IN BUDDHISM

Buddhism delves deeply into the nature of consciousness, known as *Chitta* in Pali, which forms the core of our being. Cultivating *Adhi Chitta*, or higher consciousness, is a fundamental aspect of Buddhist practice and a gateway to human excellence. When our consciousness achieves a state of focused yet relaxed awareness, it is believed that we will progress toward the four roads to power or *Iddhipada*.

The Buddha highlighted consciousness's swift and ever-changing nature, emphasizing its transient quality. It is the cornerstone of meditation, urging Buddhists to contemplate its dynamic essence. Described in Buddhist texts, a moment of consciousness, or *Chitta Khana*, is so fleeting that it is compared to a billionth part of a lightning flash. Exploring consciousness unveils our potential for excellence as it shapes our character.

Buddhism distinguishes between higher and lower human natures based on the evolution of consciousness. Traits such as greediness (*Raga Charita*), hatred (*Dosa Charita*), dullness (*Mohat Charita*), faithfulness (*Sadha Charita*), intelligence

(*Buddhi Charita*), mindfulness (*Vitakka Charita*) indicate one's character. A refined character reflects an elevated consciousness, demonstrated through generosity, sharing, and compassion.

GENEROSITY

The concept of Dana, or generosity, is a gauge of consciousness. Genuine compassion leads to egoism's dissolution, refining consciousness and character. According to Buddhism, the intention behind charitable acts holds greater significance than the act itself. Therefore, noble consciousness and character, which pave the path toward excellence, are characterized by generosity, morality (*Sheela*), and mental development (*Bhavana*). These qualities propel individuals toward enlightened living.

UNLOCKING EXCELLENCE: THE BUDDHIST PRINCIPLE OF DETACHMENT

In pursuing excellence, Buddhism reveals a profound truth: mastery arises from complete detachment in action. Yet, our fixation on outcomes ensnares us, trapping our minds in worries and attachments. We fret over success, failure, and potential results, limiting our ability to perform at our best. Entrapped in this cycle, we fail to unleash our inherent brilliance.

We can only transcend these constraints and reach our fullest potential by embracing detachment. When we release our grasp on expectations and desires, we liberate ourselves to act with unparalleled freedom and creativity. Detachment empowers us to approach every task with abandon, unburdened by concerns for outcomes.

Hence, cultivating detachment in every facet of our lives is the first secret to achieving excellence. Doing so unlocks a profound sense of peace amidst even the most demanding endeavors. Embracing detachment, we effortlessly attain excellence and fulfill our inherent potential.

CHAPTER 9

Principles for Excellence: A Path to Personal and Spiritual Growth

The principles outlined in Buddhism provide a comprehensive guide for living a life of excellence and attaining enlightenment. Let us break down some of these key concepts:

1. **Four Bodhisattva Actions:** These actions—*dana* (charity), *priya-vachana* (affectionate speech), *artha-kriyata* (beneficial conduct), and *samanarthata* (cooperation)—emphasize virtues like generosity, kindness, benefiting others, and teamwork, which are essential for personal and collective growth.

2. **Four Ways of Divine Living:** *Maitri* (friendliness), *karuna* (compassion), *mudita* (empathetic joy), and *upeksha* (equanimity) promote positive attitudes toward oneself and others, fostering harmony and well-being.

3. **Four Sublime Attitudes (Brahma-vihara):** *Metta* (loving-kindness), *karuna* (compassion), *mudita* (sympathetic joy), and *upeksha* (equanimity) cultivate boundless love, compassion, joy, and equanimity toward all beings, nurturing spiritual growth and liberation.

4. **Overcoming Five Fetters:** Buddhism addresses five negative aspects—belief in individuality, doubtfulness, over-clinging

to rites and rituals, craving and desire, and hatred—which hinder spiritual progress and enlightenment.

5. **Overcoming Five Hindrances to Excellence:** These hindrances—over-excessive desire, ill-will, laziness, restlessness, and doubt— obstruct personal and professional growth but can be overcome through mindfulness, self-awareness, and cultivation of positive qualities.

In pursuing excellence, Buddhism guides us to further wisdom for being excellent in every way. Buddhist scriptures discuss the five virtues: faith, mindfulness, energy, concentration, and wisdom. Concentrating on these virtues makes excellence a natural by-product.

Further, Buddhist scriptures discuss the six perfections or paramitas, i.e., the sutra on perfect wisdom. These six perfections or paramitas are:

1. Perfect charity or *dāna*,
2. Perfect observation of the precepts and disciplinary code, which is *śīla*,
3. Perfect effort and perseverance, which is *śanti*, or enduring patience,

4. Perfect energy or *vīrya*, which implies progress made through zeal and application,
5. Perfect meditation or *dhyāna*, and
6. Perfect wisdom or *prajñā*.

To achieve true excellence, it is essential to cultivate tranquility and calmness of spirit and mind. Achieving a balanced mental state requires stability and stillness. In Buddhism, there are six procedures for attaining *samatha*, or tranquility of being:

1. **Understanding Mistakes:** Recognizing and understanding one's mistakes and discerning good and bad deeds.

2. **Seeking Remedies:** Understanding the remedies available to rectify these mistakes.

3. **Applying Remedies:** Actively apply remedies to correct mistakes and mistakes.

4. **Attaining Stillness:** Cultivating complete stillness and quietness, thereby reaching an innocent state from which one's inner potential can fully manifest.

5. **Practicing Diligently:** Conducting diligent practice to attain mental stillness and quietude.

6. **Achieving Tranquility:** Finally reaching the state of *samatha* or tranquility and abiding within it, experiencing profound peace and calmness.

CHAPTER 10

The Path to Excellence: Insights from the Buddha

Excellence, the pursuit of mastery and fulfillment in all aspects of life, is a goal cherished by individuals striving for personal growth and development. The timeless teachings of the Buddha offer invaluable insights into the nature of excellence and guide how to cultivate it in our lives.

Siddhartha Gautam, known as the Buddha, exemplified excellence in his pursuit of enlightenment and left behind a legacy of wisdom that continues to inspire countless individuals seeking to achieve greatness. At the heart of the Buddha's teachings is the recognition of suffering (*dukkha*) as an inherent aspect of human existence. However, he also emphasized that suffering arises from attachment and craving, which can be transcended through the cessation of desire and the cultivation of wisdom, virtue, and compassion. This forms the foundation of the Four Noble Truths, which outline the nature of suffering, its causes, its cessation, and the path to its cessation.

The path prescribed by the Buddha, known as the Noble Eightfold Path, offers practical guidance on how to live a life of excellence and virtue. This path comprises eight interconnected principles, including right understanding, right intention, right speech, right action, right livelihood, right effort, right mindfulness, and right concentration. By cultivating these qualities daily, individuals can align themselves with the path of awakening and strive for excellence in all their endeavors.

Mindfulness and meditation are central Buddhist practices, offering powerful tools for cultivating excellence and mastery. Mindfulness involves non-judgmental awareness of one's thoughts, feelings, and actions, allowing individuals to cultivate clarity, focus, and self-awareness. Conversely, meditation enables practitioners to develop concentration, insight, and inner peace, providing a platform for personal growth and self-discovery.

Compassion and loving-kindness are also integral aspects of the Buddha's teachings, serving as essential components of excellence and virtue. Cultivating compassion involves empathizing with the suffering of others and actively seeking to alleviate it through acts of kindness and generosity. Loving-kindness, similarly, involves extending goodwill and benevolence toward oneself and all beings, fostering a sense of connection and unity.

In conclusion, the teachings of the Buddha offer timeless wisdom on cultivating excellence and virtue in all aspects of life. By embracing the Four Noble Truths, following the Noble Eightfold Path, cultivating mindfulness and meditation, and embodying compassion and loving-kindness, individuals can strive for excellence in their personal and spiritual growth. Ultimately, by integrating these teachings into daily life, one can realize the true potential for greatness and fulfillment that lies within each of us, achieving excellence in both worldly pursuits and the path to awakening.

CHAPTER 11

Appamāda: Diligence or Zeal in Buddhism

*A*ppamāda, often translated as diligence or zeal, is a key Buddhist concept denoting earnest and enthusiastic effort. It is the bedrock of excellence.

In Buddhist scriptures, a simile is used to emphasize the significance of diligence and zeal: "Just as the footprint of the elephant surpasses all the footprints of living beings and is considered the mightiest among them, so does zeal serve as the foundation for all meritorious qualities, standing out as the mightiest among them". The analogy emphasizes the crucial importance of diligence and zeal, which are the driving forces behind excellence (analogous to the powerful footprint of an elephant).

Buddhist commentaries highlight the connection between zeal and mindfulness, suggesting that zeal is closely associated with the presence of mindfulness (*satipatthana*). This emphasizes that a watchful and attentive state of mind is key to manifesting diligence and zeal.

In various Buddhist scriptures, including the Chapter on Zeal (*Appamáda Vagga*) in the *Dhammapada*, the Buddha emphasizes the transformative nature of zeal. In his final message, he inspires his disciples with these words: "Transient are all formations. Strive zealously!" *(Appamádena sampádetha)*.

Hence, *appamāda* is to be understood deeply. It is to become a key part of our evolution toward excellence in all spheres of life. Diligence and zeal dynamize our energies, fulfilling our lives!

CHAPTER 12

The Path of Dharma: Cultivating Excellence in Life

The Buddhist sacred texts provide detailed guidance on the activities and attitudes necessary for living a dharmic life, which inherently leads to excellence. These texts enumerate ten essentials 'dharma activities':

1. **Writing:** Sanskrit—*lekhana*, Tibetan—*yi ge 'bri pa*
2. **Worship:** Sanskrit—*puja*, Tibetan—*mchod pa*
3. **Charity:** Sanskrit—*dana*, Tibetan—*sbyin pa*
4. **Listening and Learning:** Sanskrit—*shravana*, Tibetan—*nyan ba*
5. **Reading:** Sanskrit—*vachana*, Tibetan—*klog pa*
6. **Comprehending:** Sanskrit—*udgrahana*, Tibetan—*'dzin pa*
7. **Instructing and Educating:** Sanskrit—*prakashana*, Tibetan—*rab tu ston pa*
8. **Remembering and Reciting:** Sanskrit—*svadhyaya*, Tibetan—*kha 'don byed pa*
9. **Contemplation:** Sanskrit—*chintana*, Tibetan—*sems pa*
10. **Meditation:** Sanskrit—*bhavana*, Tibetan—*sgom pa*

Additionally, the texts emphasize certain qualities essential for walking the path of excellence:

- **Desire and Zeal to Act:** *Chanda*
- **Discernment:** *Mati*
- **Right Mindfulness and Memory:** *Smriti*
- **Right Attention:** *Manaskara*
- **True Determination:** *Adhimoksha*

- **Concentration and Focus:** *Samadhi*
- **Faith:** *Shraddha*
- **Vigilance and Heedfulness:** *Apramada*
- **Calmness, Tranquility, and Serenity:** *Prashrabdhi*
- **Equanimity:** *Upeksha*
- **Decency:** *Hri*
- **Integrity and Modesty:** *Hiri*
- **Absence of Craving:** *Alobha*
- **Absence of Ill Will:** *Advesha*

By embodying these instructions, individuals naturally progress toward excellence in life.

CHAPTER 13

Buddhist Keys for Mystic and Material Excellence

THE POWER OF SPIRIT: MOVING FROM DARKNESS TO LIGHT

The essence of Buddha's message lies in awakening the power of the spirit by recognizing its eternal and infinite light (*jyoti*) within us. However, in our daily lives, we often find ourselves moving in the opposite direction, fixating on the power of the material world instead of nurturing the power of the spirit.

The power of the material is driven by desire, burdening us and preventing peace, happiness, and joy. It creates an insatiable void that material possessions can never fill. Buddha's path encourages a shift toward the subtle—an exploration of joy, a connection to the vastness of the cosmos, and an alignment with the prayerfulness of existence itself. It involves moving away from ordinary desires, thirsting for the extraordinary, and empowering the spirit within us.

While recognizing the necessity of material desires for creating value and fulfilling needs, the Buddha emphasizes the detrimental effects of wholeheartedly concentrating on the non-essential. The journey he proposes is a rebirth of desire—an evolution akin to transforming a caterpillar into a butterfly. This profound shift changes the entirety of one's being, allowing disassociation from past burdens and a flight into the subtle domains of spirituality with new wings.

Buddha's spiritual path empowers individuals by teaching them to move toward the invaluable, the immense, and the vastness that is always available provided one has the energy and will to turn away from mundane desires. It encourages a transition from material to spiritual vision, bringing silence, dispelling darkness, and reducing fear of life. It is a path that rejects the ego and material desires, offering a profound journey toward the light and essence of the spirit.

In the Buddhist view, it is not material desires that hinder spirituality but the accompanying ego that poses a challenge. While living a fulfilled material life and creating value in the world are encouraged, the emphasis is on cultivating an inner state of being that allows the experience of the light of spirit within.

This inner experience brings forth the manifestation of true value in life with enhanced power, energizing individuals in profound ways. Qualities such as clarity, vision, affection, passion, and effective communication become transformational aspects of one's being. The Buddhist perspective promotes a harmonious coexistence of material pursuits and spiritual growth, recognizing that the inner state of being holds the key to unlocking the true essence of life.

GAUTAM BUDDHA'S PATH: FROM MATERIAL TO SPIRITUAL EVOLUTION

Gautam Buddha's teachings guide us on a profound journey from material to spiritual evolution, an evolution of consciousness and desire. Mystical experiences offer endless opportunities for happiness, bliss, and joy, yet pursuing material desires often leaves us feeling unfulfilled.

Buddha's wisdom suggests an alternative approach: opening the doors to bliss and fostering transformative change within. This change involves discarding the pseudo-intelligence masquerading as worldly wisdom and aiming for spiritual awareness and inner power. This inner power is infinite, a journey deep into the sources of our being to realize the freedom of the divine enshrined within.

Self-realization creates a deeply empowering sense of peacefulness, allowing one to relax into life, move in harmony with it, and maintain enthusiasm at all levels. This shift in direction and behavior patterns eliminates the need for aggression, expands the worldview, and fosters a power within that overcomes hindrances. Gautam Buddha's path encourages a holistic and harmonious approach to life, unlocking the potential for excellence in all endeavors.

CHAPTER 14

Taoism and Buddhism

The power of softness, as emphasized in Taoism, aligns with the Buddhist idea of gentleness and yielding as a source of strength. This principle is reflected in practices like Tai Chi, where movements are soft and flowing. The Tao, often symbolized by the circle, represents the natural order of the cosmos, and embodying softness is seen as aligning with this universal flow.

The connection between Taoism (founded by Lao Tzu, who was born in China), and the path of Buddhism (founded by Gautam Buddha, who was born in Nepal), is a profound one! Both paths emphasize the essence of embracing universal intelligence within oneself. The resonance between Taoist and Buddhist ideas, of recognizing one's intrinsic enlightenment or Buddha-nature, runs deep and true. The catalyst for awakening our inherent higher energy is the individual's will to activate it, often requiring a shift in focus away from mundane cravings and desires, toward the mystical path.

By allowing the feeling of universal intelligence to penetrate the very center of the heart and mind, practitioners may experience a profound transformation. This transformation is described as surrounded by an atmosphere of great compassion and vibrancy within the soul. As a result, life moves toward a greater sense of blissfulness, joy, and fulfillment.

In essence, both Taoism and the path of Gautam Buddha encourage individuals to connect with a deeper, universal intelligence and to harmonize with the natural flow of existence. The softness and gentleness advocated in these philosophies are not signs of weakness but sources of profound strength and spiritual power.

CHAPTER 15

The Inner Conquest: Unlocking Fulfillment and True Leadership on the Path of Gautam Buddha

As human beings, a pervasive sense of dissatisfaction often pervades our existence, leaving us adrift without a clear sense of purpose. The teachings of Gautam Buddha illuminate a profound way forward—an inward journey toward direction and fulfillment. Gautam Buddha advocated for conquering one's inner self, emphasizing that conquering oneself from within is an unparalleled achievement. No external kingdoms, he asserted, can rival the profound lightheartedness and inner peace cultivated through this conquest.

The individual who conquers their inner being becomes a beacon of inspiration, creating an atmosphere of tranquility, value, and bliss. By honoring their inner treasures, such a person establishes a serene presence and empowers others to unearth their hidden treasures. In this way, they emerge as true leaders of humanity.

The mystic quest, as guided by Gautam Buddha, transforms the seeker into a source of blessings for themselves and all they encounter. The psycho-spiritual energy they radiate becomes a gift to others, fostering an environment of calm and profound value. The secret to creating enduring value lies in redirecting our focus from material desires and turning toward the perpetual bliss and light inherent within our hearts and spirits. Through this internal shift, we unearth great power and emerge victorious in life's journey. A simple resolution and an unwavering intensity to redirect our search initiate a natural process of inner discipline.

UNVEILING THE ESSENCE: A MYSTIC PERSPECTIVE ON TRUE FULFILLMENT

The predicament of humanity lies in our upbringing as egos, a pattern extending even to children who, immersed in societal and educational systems, adopt the ways of the ego. In stark contrast, the path of the Buddha advocates a profound shift—a call to deepen our connection with love, empathy, and peace while loosening the ties with ego, selfishness, jealousy, and violence. While these ideals may seem impractical in a materialistic world, they embody the only enduring values, creating a positive ripple effect that transcends the mundane.

This transformative journey is not about virtue, duty, or service; instead, it is about first embracing your true self in its purest state and sharing the inherent goodness within you. By doing so, life naturally unfolds toward successful fulfillment, empowering the spirit without needing formal statements of purpose to yourself.

Genuine fulfillment, according to the teachings of Buddha, necessitates embracing the natural path of mysticism. We fall short of reaching our highest potential without incorporating these universal values. Being interconnected with the divinity of existence allows us to rise mystically, reaching spiritual and mystical heights and illuminating our being. This touch of subtle spirituality becomes the key to unlocking a luminous and glowing inner self, paving the way for a life of profound fulfillment.

THE MYSTIC LIGHTNESS OF BEING: EMBRACING BUDDHA'S PATH TO FULFILLMENT

Embarking on the path of mysticism, as taught by Buddha, is integral to achieving genuine fulfillment in life. This journey involves feeling mystically light, deeply connected to the divinity of existence, and soaring into the beautiful realms of spiritual realization. The touch of subtle spirituality is crucial for unlocking our highest potential.

Buddha's teachings always echo a call for a light simplicity and genuine friendliness, in our approach to people and life. While seriousness holds its place, a sense of lightness of being is equally vital on the path he envisioned. This lightness, emanating from both heart and mind, leads to a spontaneous celebration of life. Within this joyous state, a positive energy of the present moment emerges, providing fertile ground for profound intellectual realizations, enhanced creativity, and a harmonious synthesis between the material and spiritual dimensions of existence.

Ultimately, the essence lies in achieving a true synthesis between the material and spiritual realms—a mystical message embedded in Buddha's teachings. By achieving this synthesis, we cultivate value within ourselves and become beacons of light for others. As we ignite our own souls and grasp the potency of the spirit, we inspire those who believe in us. This, at its core, unveils the mystic secret of leadership.

CHAPTER 16

Pathways to Enlightenment

EMBRACING 11 POSITIVE MENTAL ATTITUDES IN YOGACHARA BUDDHISM

It is good to delve into the teachings of the Yogachara School of Buddhism, which advocates 11 essential mental attitudes conducive to enlightenment and excellence. These attitudes encompass faith, modesty, lack of craving, absence of ill will, freedom from delusion, vigor, serenity, mindfulness, equanimity, mental flexibility, and a commitment to non-harm. Cultivating these qualities paves a swifter journey toward an enlightened and harmonious way of living.

THE DEPTHS OF BUDDHIST MINDFULNESS: CULTIVATING TRANQUILITY AND INSIGHT FOR SPIRITUAL COURAGE

We must deeply explore Buddhism's insights into the mind, delineating two fundamental types of mental development: *Samatha Bhavana* (tranquility) and *Vipassana Bhavana* (insight). *Samatha Bhavana* directs us toward inner peace, unyielding purity, and a focused mind, fostering sensations of clarity, happiness, and courage. Conversely, *Vipassana Bhavana* involves nurturing insight into life's impermanence, leading to heightened courage and a deeper connection with spiritual reality. The Buddha's wisdom underscores the significance of mental concentration, revealing its alignment with the truth of reality.

NAVIGATING THE PATH TO HIGHER EXCELLENCE: UNDERSTANDING THE SIX ROOT AFFLICTIONS IN THE YOGACHARA SCHOOL OF BUDDHISM

The teachings of the Yogachara School of Buddhism illuminate the six root afflictions, formidable barriers hindering the pursuit of higher excellence. These factors include an excessive attraction to sensuality, anger, spiritual ignorance, ego, pride, doubt, and wrong perceptions. Vigilance in recognizing and eliminating these factors from our mindset enhances our capacity to progress toward excellence in all aspects of life.

CONTENTMENT AND NOBILITY: THE ESSENCE OF BUDDHIST LIVING

Buddhism teaches us the profound lesson of contentment, emphasizing the cultivation of noble qualities. The Buddhist term for nobleness, '*ariyata*,' encapsulates this concept, encouraging individuals to find delight in meditation, practice detachment, and loving-kindness, and embrace simplicity in clothing and lifestyle.

Buddhist teachings highlight the importance of simplicity as a path to true nobility. This principle is exemplified by figures like Steve Jobs, who chose to live simply despite achieving immense success. The journey to enlightenment, described as a series of small steps, involves understanding the transient nature of material enjoyment, much like waves that rise and disappear on the ocean.

Living in harmony with the Buddhist doctrine of impermanence allows for a conscious and noble existence. Embracing this perspective fosters inner peace and contentment, guiding us toward a more meaningful and enlightened life.

CHAPTER 17

Emulating the Bodhisattvas for Excellence

SIGNS OF BUDDHAHOOD

Buddhahood manifests through distinct symptoms. This state is characterized by a tranquil mind, an internal sense of unity, heightened love, and spontaneous joy. Worry dissipates, paving the way for deep relaxation and calmness. While these are markers on the mystic path, they offer valuable lessons for practical living. Embracing deep relaxation, calmness, and love from the Bodhisattva's signs can profoundly impact our lives.

Imbibing Lessons

Allow thoughts to subside, let love to guide your actions, and discover causeless joy in every experience. Recognize the cosmic truth radiating from everything and connect with it. Doing so, you align your being with the universe's harmony and rhythm, fostering true personal growth. Achieve wholeheartedness and genuine enjoyment in both work and personal life. As the passages of the heart and mind become clearer, your being becomes a conduit for great power and energy.

The Challenge of Modern Life

Modern life saturates individuals with information, thoughts, and entertainment, leaving little space. A diminished space of consciousness hinders the flow of greater power. The fundamental lessons from the Bodhisattva encourage a shift in thought patterns, facilitating a more effortless connection to the power of consciousness. The teachings of Buddha offer a powerful means not only to improve oneself but also to contribute to building a better society and civilization.

LIVING THE BUDDHA'S TEACHINGS

Rediscovering Purity

In these times, the teachings of Buddha are essential. Emulating the Buddhas involves shedding old behavior patterns and returning to a state of purity, your original Buddhahood. This state brings a sense of life as a blessing, fostering deep gratitude, joy, and meaningful, anxiety-free living. Every action becomes a blessing, impacting yourself and everyone you touch with your work and words.

Imbibing Buddha's Qualities

Embracing Buddha's qualities opens the gateway to profound life experiences. It's about entering the heart space, perceiving things in a brighter light, and understanding the heart of reality within yourself. Life transforms into a joyful adventure to be navigated without conditions. This perspective revitalizes your spirit, bringing freshness, youthfulness, and sensitivity. Operating from this integrated, happy state empowers individuals to find great happiness and overcome challenges in work and relationships.

Overcoming Predicaments

Life presents numerous predicaments and challenging choices. However, functioning from a state of Buddhahood, characterized by inner purity of consciousness, equips individuals to manage challenges effectively. It's akin to the sun's rays dispelling the darkness of the night. Although challenges may return, the energy cultivated from this state allows for overcoming hurdles with renewed hope and creativity.

Buddhahood Unveiled

The essence of Buddhahood lies in clearing the skies of consciousness from mists and clouds. Life's purpose is to function optimally, to reach your alpha state, allowing the hidden Buddha within to manifest. While everyone carries hidden treasures, embracing the qualities of a Buddha enables these treasures to reveal themselves. Thus, absorb the virtues of the Bodhisattva and become a vessel for the divine music resonating across the cosmos.

Breaking Free from Conditioning

Shift your perspective away from conditioned thinking and auto-hypnosis. Buddhism urges a departure from entrenched beliefs and philosophies, encouraging entry into a state of awareness—the heart of wisdom. Acting in loving awareness, often termed 'mindfulness' in the modern age, involves transcending the mind's constant chatter. It's a journey into the formless, indefinable aspects of your being, where great courage emerges, allowing you to sing your unique song and dance your spiritual dance in this lifetime.

Embracing Limited Time

Given time constraints, seize each moment to sing your song and dance your dance. In doing so, you discover a profound freedom intrinsic to your nature. This freedom leads to realizing your truth, potential, divinity, and love. Feeling a part of eternity epitomizes the fundamental attitude of the Bodhisattva's behavior.

Harmony in the Face of Challenges

The Bodhisattva's principal trait is an unwavering resilience against offense. They let events unfold without internalizing hurt or offense. This stance maintains a continuous connection with universal truth, fostering a life of profound joy and inner bliss. By embodying this spontaneity, one transcends the sense of struggle, entering a realm of freedom, shedding anxiety, and rising above personal affronts. This shift unleashes a powerful force, transforming one into a charismatic source of healing energy for oneself and others.

Alchemy of Consciousness

Like an alchemist, the Buddha transforms consciousness's base material into gold. This symbolic expression underscores how the fundamental attitude within oneself can manifest tangible outcomes through action. The Bodhisattva's spontaneity detaches from the conditioned and homogeneous mindset of the majority, fostering an authentic journey that overcomes fears, especially the fear of insecurity. Acting from a secure innermost core results in total action, distinct from partial actions undertaken without such deep connection.

The Power of Love and Compassion

The profound secret lies in cultivating a love so deep, compassion so vast, and empathy so genuine that not only does one's spirit evolve, but a harmonious connection with the entire world is established. Coming into tune with the world involves accepting circumstances and working through them with unwavering determination. This acceptance not only fosters self-respect but also effortlessly earns the respect of others. The very presence of an individual radiates a commanding respect, highlighting the transformative power of love and compassion.

The Essence of Presence

True respect is not merely a product of external actions but is deeply rooted in the presence, vibe, and energy one emanates. When a self-realized person enters a room, their serenity creates a magnetic field, attracting others intoxicated by this energy. This presence exudes charisma and leadership qualities, highlighting that respect is an inherent quality, not an external achievement. Embracing this essence from the Bodhisattva's teachings allows individuals to cultivate a powerful, serene energy that naturally draws others in.

Facing Life with Fresh Consciousness

Life is a continuous journey toward the new, and facing it requires freshness of consciousness. Unconditional preparedness for whatever happens reflects divine energy. When the ripples of incessant thoughts are stilled, one begins to function from the vastness of their inner truth, creativity, and beauty. In this state, individuals become purposeful contributors to the world, acting spontaneously and reflecting the divine essence in their actions.

CHAPTER 18

The Ultimate Mystic Principles for Excellence

1. **Transcendence of the Known:** Buddhism is portrayed as a journey into the unknown, residing within oneself as the divine spark. To truly know it, one must avoid self-suppression and refuse to define oneself within boundaries. This realization expands consciousness,

leading to clarity and the opening of the inner eye of wisdom.

2. **Flowing with Life:** Life and existence are continuous flux and flow. Buddhism advises against getting stuck in rigid ideas and attachments. The essence is to flow like life, avoiding mental entrapment and maintaining a dynamic, open attitude.

3. **Transcending the Fear of Death:** Buddhist Tantras teach the transcendence of fears, especially the fear of death. By detaching from the past and being completely present, one can overcome the fear of death, leading to spiritual joy.

4. **Being Yourself:** True happiness, peace, and stress-free living require authenticity. Being oneself, rooted in one's divine nature, is at the core of the Buddhist attitude toward attaining these states.

5. **Nurturing Buddha-Nature:** Buddha-nature is likened to a seed within, requiring nurturing

to sprout into a mighty tree. Individuals have the responsibility to nourish this seed with positive energy.

6. **Thirst for Truth:** The state of thirsting for higher truth, the *Mumukshu* state, leads to enlightenment. Starting with a genuine thirst for truth, happiness naturally follows.

7. **The Laughing Buddha:** The laughing Buddha symbolizes the ability to find joy within oneself and not take oneself too seriously. This carefree attitude and heightened awareness establish a deeper spiritual passion.

8. **Worrying about the Future:** Buddhism advises against excessive worry about the future, likening everything to footprints on the seashore eventually being washed away. Embracing carefreeness and resting in the present moment is encouraged.

9. **Non-possessiveness:** Possessiveness is considered one of the worst human qualities in Buddhism. It poisons the purity of love, leading

to various problems. Non-possessiveness is advocated as the path to happiness.

10. **Inner Guru and Experiential Knowledge:** Beyond formal study, Buddhism emphasizes turning to the inner Buddha nature for true knowledge and the transcendence of sorrow. Experiential knowledge, gained through inner guidance, is more important than scriptural knowledge.

11. **Inner Power in Aloneness:** The true test of inner power lies in the ability to be fulfilled and happy even in a state of aloneness. Finding joy in solitude is seen as walking the path of the Buddha.

12. **Beyond External Knowledge:** Visualizing and perceiving with a Buddha-like clarity is key to excellence. Buddhism suggests that gaining knowledge from external sources, like books, is secondary. The importance lies in self-realization, transcending external knowledge for spiritual discovery.

13. **Non-calculating Mind:** The enlightened mind is portrayed as non-calculating, acting out of a purity of consciousness rather than societal standards. This state leads to selfless work and the transcendence of anxiety through dynamism.

14. **Fulfillment of Desires:** The Buddhas promise that their deepest desires are always fulfilled. Buddhism emphasizes the importance of desires and seeking, encouraging individuals to be mindful of their aspirations.

15. **Underutilized Capacity for Love:** Buddhism views the ability to love and show compassion as underutilized in humans. The more this capacity is used, the stronger and happier individuals become. True happiness arises when love and compassion are practiced for their own sake.

16. **Perception of the Divine:** The perception of the divine is through inner vision. Buddhism advises not getting overly distracted by

external circumstances, encouraging conscious awareness of the inner self for true success.

17. **Going Beyond Identification:** The core of Buddhism is described as going beyond identification with the mind and body. Recognizing one's nature as unlimited pure consciousness leads to courage, removing unnecessary anxieties, and spontaneous joy and delight.

18. **Naturalness in Zen Buddhism:** Zen Buddhism advocates being natural and ordinary, unlike some religions that emphasize rituals and special ceremonies. Being natural and spontaneous allows for beautiful and productive actions.

19. **Patience and Expansion:** Impatience and anxiety are linked, and Buddhism encourages patience, relaxation, and non-anxiety. Patience expands one's entirety of being, leading to the understanding that there is sufficient time to realize one's highest potential in life.

20. **Buddhism and Beauty:** Buddhism is essentially about beauty: it emphasizes the acknowledgment of existence's beauty as a gift. According to Zen Buddhism, true intelligence is recognizing and having faith in the beauty of existence.

21. **Cultivating Friendliness:** Reiterating the importance of cultivating friendliness, Buddhism emphasizes that feeling friendliness from within makes an individual unbounded. Friendliness enables one to transcend superficial likes and dislikes, moving toward greater strength and power from within.

22. **Moral Purity and Meditative Attitude:** Moral purity is highlighted as a by-product of the meditative attitude in Buddhism. Inner meditativeness leads to inner peace, the fragrance of higher consciousness, and less egoistic functioning.

These Buddhist concepts continue to unravel the profound principles of Buddhism, guiding individuals toward self-realization, inner peace, and a harmonious relationship with existence.

CHAPTER 19

Being Full-hearted: Pour Your Heart!

Truly pouring one's heart out in whatever one does is the way of the Buddhist monk. That should also be the way for us to live and work in the so-called material world. It is a basic value for excellence: the ability to pour all our energies cleanly and purely into whatever we do in the present moment—holding nothing back, not being burdened in the head. We should go into whatever we are doing with full-heartedness and not be fragmentary. Not getting caught in the past or the future, the thoughts of which are barriers to working with a totality of energy.

So, this principle essentially implies cleansing one's consciousness completely: coming clean through, energetically and completely, no matter what one does. Through this, the dance of energy happens in a total and depthful manner. This is the way of true spirituality. But it is also a way of creating true bliss within us and value within society. It is the natural way. It is the Buddhist way. It is also the way of Tao, the way of Tantra, the way of Kabbalah, the way of old folk religions, the way of Gita and Vedanta, and the way of Kashmir Shaivism. It is the way of all mystics throughout the world. The basic implication is to live with enthusiasm. The basic quality is to work through one's ultimate nature in a manner where one is no longer restless. Holding something back always makes us restless! Letting go completely and expressing ourselves to the fullness of our energy by pouring our hearts into our acts is the way of spontaneity. It is the way of natural fulfillment. It makes you quiet within.

But what does this principle entail? How do we productively pour our hearts out in what we do? It entails the art of balance: that is what the monk and the mystics seek to inculcate within their hearts. A balanced awareness and a witnessing awareness are key. Not too much on one extreme or the other extreme: being of a nature where, even amid competition, one can retain inner bliss and quietness within the heart and mind. The miracle of potential fulfillment comes through this calmness and quietness of being. That is the divine way, leading to a harmony of energy. It leads to a situation where what you do becomes conducive to you.

Eventually, your work should not conflict with your heart and mind. Conversely, your heart and mind should not conflict with your work. You can integrate the two, but it requires that you be deeply conscious, to an extent where you can be on a spiritual plane within your consciousness. And yet retain the ability to work effectively on the material plane. This idea is at the heart of Zen Buddhist philosophy. This is at the heart of what somebody like Steve Jobs sought to inculcate within Apple Computer: a clean aesthetic, with people working extremely hard, with a completeness of energy, but at the same time giving heed to the inner quality of deep product aesthetics. In doing so, the product comes out to have all those qualities of true value.

The way we are within is the way we manifest material things. So, to materially manifest good things, we must be in a state of consciousness that is conducive to that. This is the new paradigm of leadership. This is the new paradigm of innovation. It is not to be a destructive force. Yes, in humanity's past, it has been seen that much of science and technology has been a product of man's quest for violence, his fighting wars, and so on. But for a sustainable future, it is imperative that technology work in tandem with the virtues of inward balance and calmness. Only then can the world be balanced. Why is there so much ecological imbalance in the world, so much imbalance in terms of wealth, so much imbalance in terms of prosperity? So much violence, conflict, and so on? The inner and greater luminosity of being is missing from man's heart. And that is what Buddhism seeks to teach. It is not about destructiveness. The new paradigm is about creativeness. Creativity is not just a very gross material manner but also a creative attitude:

the aesthetic attitude within the hearts and minds of individuals.

So, the first experience has to be within: out of that will come all good things in our material work, too. Unless we make this attitude of inner cultivation of virtue a bedrock of our beings, we cannot move toward peace. What you are within symbolizes what you will manifest outside yourself. Only a person of bliss will manifest bliss. Only a person of creativity will manifest creativity within the world. So, that is enough if you are luminous with it within yourself. Then, whatever you do will have a positive vibe and will be able to influence hearts and minds well. Hence, the question of spirituality—especially Eastern spirituality—is significant. It is not about 'God' but an attitude to life. It is about the way you make the ordinary extraordinary. The way you transcend your inner states and transmute them into something higher, something with higher quality.

In the view of Buddhism, form and formlessness are complementary. You may want to give something form in the real world (as a product or service, perhaps), but the formless qualities within yourself give birth to that form that you want. This is a remarkably interesting and defining characteristic of Buddhism: the concept of formlessness being the basis of form. And this is what Buddhism says about the universe: out of formlessness comes the form of the cosmos and the universe! So, this understanding is at the heart of the creative search, and through this understanding comes a great revolution in heart and mind. Then you see that it is not about manufacturing things on the outer; it is actually about manufacturing a state of being itself—and not manufacturing, but simply being in your natural spiritual state. This leads to creating something great within the world through you. If, on the other hand, there is a dullness or deep unconsciousness within the human soul, it cannot possibly attain great peaks in the material world either. This is a natural phenomenon. It is a corollary which follows natural logic. Hence, all that is truly achieved is through the effortless action of inner transformation: inner bliss, inner joy, and so on. That creates ripples in your outer action. That is the foundation of your being itself, which can create the quantum leaps needed for you to function with great value within the world. All our work is eventually of no value from the cosmic perspective. Yet it is the spiritual value imbued in it that gives it meaning.

Mystic 'pouring of heart' is a question of using more than your five senses: it is about using that sixth sense—that super sense—which is the sense of spirituality. That is what invokes the subtle sense of the divine. Through it, you start looking at things with a divine eye. When you do that, you feel a great euphoria in what you do. And if you feel euphoria in what you do, you can create things with a totality of energy and great passion. You can create blissfulness within the world.

Hidden within the deep core of ourselves is a great ability to be phenomenally creative and productive. Yet few people can do it, and this is simply because there is something wrong with how they look at the question of consciousness. Now, religion has become relegated to the search for 'God,' but it is a search to manage and unlock what is already within us in our consciousness. There is no need to search for an outer God. The Buddhist's viewpoint may seem odd to somebody from another path because the search is quite different. It is about finding the blissful dance and vibration of virtue within us and not so much about an outer

God. Within oneself is godliness, says Buddhism. And that is its utter beauty. That is its prayer. The interior-most is considered in Buddhism to be the transcendent and brilliant self. That enriches you at every level: material, spiritual, etc. If that is going correct, everything goes correct. Hence, to improve upon what you are doing (work, relationships, leadership, team roles, etc.), it is always about first being able to relate to yourself in the deepest possible manner. To go deeply into the mystical intoxication of inner bliss and allow it to tranquilize you into a state of calmness, a state of balance, a state of such utter coolness that you can walk the journey in a far brisker and more efficient manner!

Life is a journey, be it material life or spiritual life. It is the quality of *how* we are making the journey that makes the whole thing meaningful or not. If we walk the path with joy and the totality of our inner energy (coupled with clarity of consciousness), we would then find that we are rather effortlessly and spontaneously able to manifest more and more good things through the instrument of our mind-bodies. So, all that is needed is what happens within the consciousness within the heart. To be able to put its absolute best qualities into whatever we do.

And to cut out of the mind those ideas that are counterfeit and not needed, which are the result of the various conditions of society. And when you do that, when you cut conditioning out, you attain a state where you become purer and stronger. Chip away at the unessential, and you will reach the essential. Michelangelo, the artist, was once asked what the secret of his creativity was when it came to sculpture. He said he just keeps chipping away those parts of the marble that are not needed, and what eventually remains is the pure beauty of the statue! It is spontaneous. And Buddhism is like that: it calls us to chip away at unnecessary things. And then what remains is your very essence. What remains is your very purity of consciousness. That itself has immense power. That itself has the means to bring you the totality of freedom. You don't need 'God' for that. And that is why Buddhism is so beautiful: it says we can bring about this state within ourselves. All it requires is non-resistance. All it requires is a little faith that we can do it! Plus, you have some guts to pour your heart into what you do. Then, you can go beyond your ordinary self and find an even higher quality of life.

CHAPTER 20

Three Teachings for Excellence

UNLOCKING INNER STRENGTH: THE FIVE POWERS OF TRUE SPIRITUALITY IN BUDDHISM

Delve into the essence of true spirituality through Buddhism's emphasis on realizing our innate powers, known as *Bala* in Pali. Five pivotal powers—faith (*Shraddhabala*), energy/effort (*Viryabala*), mindfulness (*Smritibala*), concentration (*Samadhibala*), and wisdom (*Paññābala*)—are highlighted for their significance. The unshakeable nature of each power is revealed: faith resists hopelessness, energy combats laziness, mindfulness prevails over forgetfulness, concentration overcomes destructiveness, and wisdom triumphs over ignorance. Correct intentions, mindfulness, meditation, and efforts nurture the growth of these powers, fostering spontaneous courage and fearlessness in our lives.

NAVIGATING HIGHER EXCELLENCE: INSIGHTS FROM THE YOGACHARA SCHOOL OF BUDDHISM

The Yogachara School of Buddhism enlightens us about the six root afflictions: the factors that hinder our path to higher excellence. Vigilance against these factors is essential. They include an excessive attraction toward sensuality, heightened anger, spiritual ignorance, ego and pride, excessive doubt, and wrong perception. Eliminating these factors from our mindset enhances our ability to excel in all our pursuits.

THE MIDDLE PATH IN BUDDHISM: BALANCING LIFE'S EXTREMES

The beauty of Buddhism lies in its teaching of the Middle Path, known as *Majjhima Patipada* in Pali. This path advocates for avoiding the extremes of life—whether indulging in sensual pleasures (*kamasukhallikanuyoga*) or engaging in self-mortification (*attakilamathanuyoga*). It teaches us to be gentle yet disciplined, finding balance in our actions. Understanding the Middle Path is central to the Buddha's concept of *Dharma*. Embracing this spiritual journey leads to spontaneous excellence in life, making it a key teaching for achieving excellence in Buddhism.

CHAPTER 21

Buddhism's Essence: A Path to Excellence

In today's complex world, the profound wisdom of Buddhism often gets lost in a maze of cultural adaptations and esoteric terminology. This chapter aims to distill the core teachings of Buddhism into accessible, practical guidance for modern life. By focusing on the fundamental principles that transcend specific schools or traditions, we can uncover a universal approach to personal growth and excellence.

THE CORNERSTONE OF OPENNESS

At the heart of Buddhist philosophy lies the concept of openness (akutillatta or vyayattata). This principle encourages us to approach life with an expansive mindset, free from the constraints of narrow thinking. Openness is not merely an intellectual exercise but a holistic approach that encompasses both the mind and heart.

By cultivating openness, we unlock the potential for true freedom and tap into the infinite treasures life has to offer. This radical approach places openness above all else, including rituals, prayers, or religious hierarchies. It's through this unbound state that we can delve deeper into our innate divine nature and connect with the foundational aspects of existence.

The Buddhist perspective posits that our deepest yearnings are, in essence, a thirst for cosmic splendor. By embracing openness, we create a direct channel to this universal wellspring, allowing us to experience the luminous grace of the transcendent.

This state of being goes beyond conventional notions of morality or religious dogma, focusing instead on the spontaneous unfolding of truth and perception.

PRACTICAL APPLICATIONS OF OPENNESS

1. **Cultivate Spontaneity:** Allow yourself to respond to life's situations without the burden of preconceived notions or judgments.

2. **Embrace the Present Moment:** Practice mindfulness in everyday activities, whether tending to a garden, engaging in conversation, or focusing on work tasks.

3. **Challenge Your Assumptions:** Regularly question your beliefs and be willing to revise them in light of new experiences or information.

4. **Seek New Experiences:** Step out of your comfort zone and expose yourself to diverse perspectives and ways of life.

INTUITION AND THE
POETIC VISION OF LIFE

Buddhism emphasizes the importance of intuition as a means of accessing deeper truths. This intuitive capacity is described as a more poetic vision of life, allowing us to perceive subtle harmonies within ourselves and our connection to the divine energy that permeates the universe.

To cultivate this intuitive wisdom:

1. **Practice Meditation:** Regular meditation helps quiet the analytical mind and enhances our capacity for intuitive insights.

2. **Engage in Creative Activities:** Artistic pursuits can help bypass the logical mind and tap into intuitive knowledge.

3. **Trust Your Inner Voice:** Learn to distinguish between the chatter of the ego and the quieter, more profound intuitive guidance.

4. **Observe Nature:** Spending time in nature can attune us to the rhythms and patterns of the universe, enhancing our intuitive abilities.

THE COURAGE TO
EMBRACE THE UNKNOWN

Buddhist teachings encourage us to venture beyond the familiar and comfortable. This willingness to explore the unknown is essential for personal growth and the realization of our full potential. It requires courage to step away from institutionalized learning, religious dogma, and limiting self-concepts.

To cultivate this courage:

1. **Take Calculated Risks:** Regularly push yourself to try new things, even if they seem daunting at first.

2. **Embrace Uncertainty:** Learn to find comfort in not knowing all the answers and view uncertainty as an opportunity for growth.

3. **Practice Non-attachment:** Develop the ability to let go of outcomes and focus on the process of growth and exploration.

4. **Cultivate Resilience:** Build your capacity to bounce back from setbacks and view challenges as opportunities for learning.

TRANSCENDING DUALITY

A key aspect of Buddhist philosophy is the transcendence of dualistic thinking. This involves moving beyond rigid categorizations of good and bad, pleasure and pain, heaven and hell. By adopting a more holistic perspective, we can relate to all aspects of life with equanimity and grace.

Practices for transcending duality:

1. **Mindfulness of Thoughts:** Observe your thoughts without judgment, recognizing that they are not absolute truths.

2. **Cultivate Equanimity:** Practice maintaining a balanced state of mind in the face of both pleasant and unpleasant experiences.

3. **Embrace Paradox:** Learn to hold seemingly contradictory ideas simultaneously, recognizing that truth often lies beyond simple either/or propositions.

4. **Practice Non-judgment:** Cultivate the ability to observe without immediately categorizing experiences as good or bad.

THE CATHARTIC JOURNEY OF SELF-DISCOVERY

Buddhism recognizes that the path to enlightenment often involves confronting repressed emotions and unconscious patterns. This process can be challenging but ultimately liberating, as it allows us to integrate all aspects of our being.

Strategies for navigating this inner journey:

1. **Shadow Work:** Explore and integrate the aspects of yourself that you typically hide or reject.

2. **Emotional Intelligence:** Hone one's ability to more clearly understand and manage one's emotions, in a manner that is effective.

3. **Therapy or Counseling:** Consider professional support to help navigate complex emotional terrain.

4. **Journaling:** Use writing as a tool to explore your inner landscape and gain insights into your thoughts and feelings.

DISIDENTIFICATION
FROM MENTAL CHATTER

Buddhism teaches that while the mind is a valuable tool, it should not be the sole arbiter of our experience. By learning to step back from the constant stream of thoughts, we can access a more expansive state of being.

Techniques for disidentification:

1. **Meditation:** Regular practice helps create space between our thoughts and our sense of self.

2. **Mindfulness:** Cultivate present-moment awareness throughout daily activities.

3. **Self-Inquiry:** Ask yourself, "Who is the one thinking these thoughts?" to create distance from mental activity.

4. **Witness Consciousness:** Practice observing your thoughts and emotions as if you were a neutral spectator.

OVERCOMING UNWHOLESOME TRAITS

Buddhist philosophy identifies three primary obstacles to excellence and fulfillment: greed (Lobha), hate (Dosha), and delusion (Moha). By working to transcend these unwholesome traits, we can cultivate a more balanced and harmonious existence.

Practices for overcoming unwholesome traits:

1. **Generosity:** Counter greed by regularly practicing acts of giving and cultivating contentment.

2. **Loving-kindness:** Develop compassion and empathy to counteract hatred and ill-will.

3. **Wisdom:** Cultivate clear seeing and understanding to dispel delusion and ignorance.

4. **Ethical Living:** Adhere to principles of right conduct to create a foundation for spiritual growth.

CONTEMPLATING
IMPERMANENCE

The Buddhist concept of anicca-saññá, or the perception of impermanence, is a powerful tool for shifting our perspective and priorities. By regularly contemplating the transitory nature of all phenomena, including our own lives, we can cultivate a sense of urgency and focus on what truly matters.

Ways to contemplate impermanence:

1. **Death Meditation:** Regularly reflect on the inevitability of death to clarify your priorities and values.

2. **Observe Change:** Pay attention to the constant flux in nature, relationships, and your own body and mind.

3. **Practice Letting Go:** Cultivate non-attachment by regularly releasing things, ideas, or habits that no longer serve you.

4. **Gratitude Practice:** Appreciate the present moment, recognizing that nothing lasts forever.

CONCLUSION:
THE PATH TO EXCELLENCE

By integrating these core Buddhist principles into our lives, we can cultivate a state of being that naturally tends toward excellence. This approach is not about striving for perfection or adhering to rigid rules, but rather about aligning ourselves with the fundamental nature of reality and our own innate potential.

The Buddhist path to excellence involves:

1. Cultivating openness in heart and mind
2. Developing intuition and a poetic vision of life
3. Embracing the unknown with courage
4. Transcending dualistic thinking
5. Engaging in the cathartic journey of self-discovery
6. Disidentifying from mental chatter
7. Overcoming unwholesome traits
8. Contemplating impermanence

By embracing these principles, we can navigate life with greater wisdom, compassion, and effectiveness. This approach not only leads to personal fulfillment but also contributes to the well-being of all beings, aligning with the highest ideals of Buddhist philosophy.

Remember, the path to excellence is not a destination but a continuous journey of growth and discovery. Each moment offers an opportunity to embody these teachings and move closer to our highest potential. As we integrate these principles into our daily lives, we become living examples of the transformative power of Buddhist wisdom, inspiring others and contributing to the collective evolution of consciousness.

There never was, there never will be,
nor is there a person now
who is wholly blamed or wholly praised.

—Gautam Buddha (In the context of excellence, this quote reminds us that perfection is an illusion. True excellence isn't about achieving flawless performance or universal acclaim, but rather about continuous growth and balanced self-improvement. It encourages us to strive for progress without being paralyzed by the fear of criticism or inflated by excessive praise.)

When the iron bird flies
and horses run on wheels,
the dharma will travel!

—Guru Padmasambhava i.e. Guru Rinpoche, or 'Precious Guru' (This prophecy of his, when viewed through the lens of excellence, speaks to the adaptability and enduring relevance of Buddhist wisdom. It suggests that the path to excellence is not static but evolves with technological and societal changes. Excellence in the modern world requires us to integrate timeless wisdom with contemporary knowledge and tools.)

OM TARE TUTTARE TURE SVAHA
OM MANI PADME HUM

These mantras, in the context of excellence, serve as powerful tools for mental focus and spiritual alignment. "Om Tare Tuttare Ture Svaha" (The Tara Mantra) is associated with overcoming obstacles and fears. In pursuing excellence, it reminds us to face challenges with courage and determination.

"Om Mani Padme Hum" embodies the transformation of the rough material of our lives into something precious. In terms of excellence, it represents the ongoing process of refining our thoughts, actions, and being into their highest forms.

By incorporating these elements, we underscore that excellence in Buddhism is not just about external achievements, but about internal transformation, adaptability to change, balanced self-assessment, and the cultivation of wisdom and compassion. The journey toward excellence is ongoing, shaped by timeless principles yet responsive to the ever-changing world around us.

Acknowledgments

I would like to express my sincere gratitude to the individuals who have played a pivotal role in bringing this series to life: Anuj Bahri, my exceptional literary agent at Red Ink; Gaurav Sabharwal and Shantanu Duttagupta, my outstanding publishers at Fingerprint! Publishing, along with their dedicated team. Special thanks to Shilpa Mohan, my editor for her invaluable contributions.

I would also like to extend my heartfelt appreciation to my parents, Anita and Captain Jeet Gupta, for their unwavering support throughout this journey. To my beloved sister, Priti and brother-in-law, Manish Goel, thank you for always being there for me. My niece, Vaanee and nephew, Kartikay, have been a constant source of joy and inspiration and I am grateful for their presence in my life.

I am truly humbled by the collective efforts and encouragement from all these remarkable individuals, without whom this series would not have been possible.

Pranay is a renowned mystic, captivating speaker and accomplished author who has dedicated his life to exploring the depths of spirituality. With a deep understanding of the human experience and an unwavering commitment to personal growth, Pranay has written numerous books that offer insights into the realms of spirituality.

One of Pranay's most celebrated contributions is his groundbreaking series of modules titled "Advanced Spirituality for Leadership and Success." His transformative PowerTalks and MysticTalks have garnered international recognition for their exceptional ability to inspire and empower individuals from all walks of life. Pranay's unique approach combines ancient wisdom with contemporary insights, providing a roadmap for achieving spiritual fulfillment while embracing leadership qualities that lead to remarkable success.

To learn more about Pranay and his transformative teachings, visit his official website at pranay.org.

To buy more books by the author scan the QR code given below.